COMPASSIONATE
SALES

COMPASSIONATE SALES

CULTIVATING CUSTOMER LOYALTY

Tashi Maldonado

ISBN-13: 9781530825714
ISBN-10: 1530825717
Library of Congress Control Number: 2016905352
CreateSpace Independent Publishing Platform
North Charleston, South Carolina

TABLE OF CONTENTS

Part 1   The Career You Chose · · · · · · · · 1
          A Special Breed · · · · · · · · · · · · 3
          A Great Responsibility · · · · · · · · 6

Part 2   It Starts with You · · · · · · · · · · · 11
          Breaking Down the Walls · · · · · 12
          Get Real · · · · · · · · · · · · · · · · · 19
          The Evil Twins · · · · · · · · · · · · · 29
          It's Right in the Word · · · · · · · 36

Part 3   Sustainable Partnerships · · · · · 39
          Hidden Costs · · · · · · · · · · · · · · 40
          Real vs. Fake · · · · · · · · · · · · · 45
          Trust You Me · · · · · · · · · · · · · · 64

Vulnerability is not winning or losing; it's having the courage to show up and be seen when we have no control over the outcome. Vulnerability is not weakness; it's our greatest measure of courage.

—Brené Brown, *Rising Strong*

PART 1

THE CAREER YOU CHOSE

A Special Breed

Salespeople. We are a special breed. Have you ever noticed how the jobs throughout your professional life have always migrated back to the sales channel? That's because it's in your blood. Sales is something that is difficult to teach the nuances of because it is inherent. Why do we do what we do? Because sales is in our DNA. I know this because my two adult children are both talented salespeople, and neither of them has had any formal sales training. It's something on a cellular level that drives us to achieve that level of interaction and rapport with others, drives us to compete, to achieve. It

3

is your arrow. In a way, we are very lucky to understand what our calling is. Many search for years for career paths that resonate with them. Not us. We've known it all along.

It's not all smooth sailing, however. Salespeople are far too familiar with the rough sides of our diamond. Like a tortured artist or a heartbroken songstress, we endure rejection and use it as motivation for our next accomplishments. We tie our personal identities to sales goals that someone else has chosen, often with no input from us. We go up against the seemingly impossible at times, and we do it with smiles on our faces.

Yes, we work in the customer service industry. Those of us in professions with high levels of customer interaction know how to walk in the door with pleasant and engaging attitudes, no matter what our days have been like. We know how to keep calm tones of voices in the most volatile of situations. It is incumbent on us to convince another person to do a certain thing—our paycheck literally depends on it. Very few career choices require this level of professionalism.

All this begs the question: what are the pitfalls that come hand in hand with these pressures? At what point are we being inauthentic in accomplishing our goals? What does doing business in an inauthentic manner cost us? What payoffs are we getting when we're not living our values, not living our best lives? Consider that last sentence carefully. We will explore these and other questions together in this book.

A Great Responsibility

Salespeople are notoriously hard on themselves. Behind the bravado masks we wear in front of contemporaries and customers lie our many insecurities. Feelings of being overwhelmed at times. Fear of being imposters. Feelings of "Who entrusted me with this job anyway? Did they really believe I could do this? I guess I'll just 'fake it till I make it.'" It's an underlying feeling of anxiety with a good dose of fear of failure.

These are common feelings felt on occasion by most people who hold great responsibility. I remember the moment when it became time for me to take my first child home from the hospital. Despite reading all the right books and taking classes during my pregnancy, as my husband and I fumbled with the car seat outside the hospital's front doors, I started to feel a sense of panic. "These people are crazy," I said. "They're just letting us take this tiny, helpless baby home, who is completely dependent on us to live, and we have no idea what we are doing."

As it turned out, I was entrusted with a great responsibility on that day, and I rose to the occasion. The truth is, if the hospital had truly had concerns about our ability to care for the child, they would have never released her to us. That insecurity resided within me at the time, and I overcame it. It's the same with kids as they mature—the more responsibilities they are given, the more accountable they tend to become.

Salespeople aren't just walking into an office and being paid the same day in and day out, regardless of the level of their efforts. They are accountable for the growth of their customer bases. They are committed to the owners of their companies to bring in those dollars. They are personally responsible for being good stewards of their companies' customer relationships. They are holders of great responsibility. Much like the baby scenario, someone has entrusted you with something. Someone believes in your talents and abilities to preserve and grow relationships with their valued and hard-earned customers. Rise to the occasion. Acknowledge your worthiness; take ownership. The good news is that if you are feeling like an imposter, it points to you doing a good job. This is counterintuitive, I know, but think of it this way: how many people who are careless and unmotivated within their jobs even think to worry about such things? It shows that you care about your performance. It matters to you. You have integrity. And most likely, you *want* to rise to the occasion and experience personal fulfillment as well as a high level of success in your career.

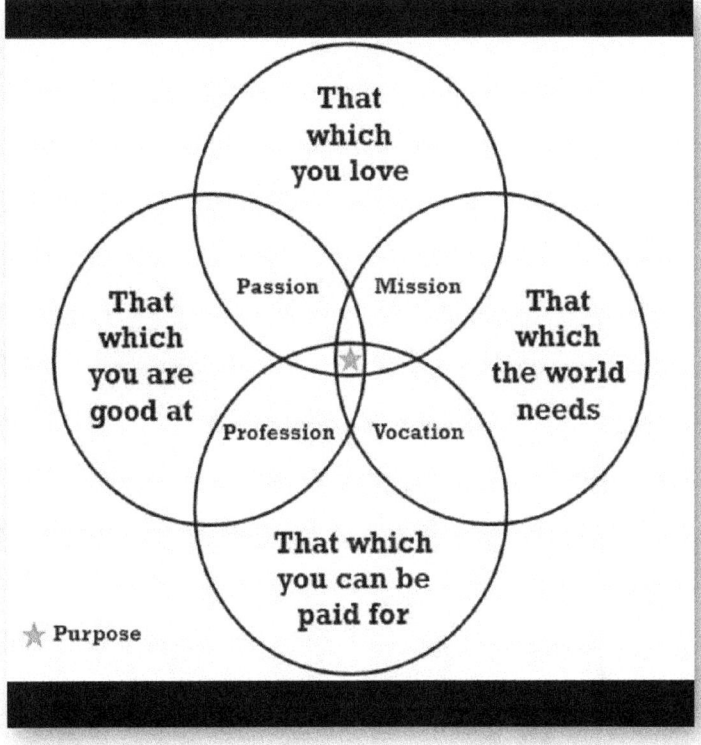

PART 2

IT STARTS WITH YOU

Breaking Down the Walls

I n this book we will not be discussing specific sales techniques. If you have worked in the sales industry for any amount of time, you've doubtlessly been exposed to and trained in various sales processes, along with their accompanying acronyms that help you remember the steps. No, this is about something different. It's about the very foundation of *presence and authentic interaction* with the customer that must take place first before you bring a sales technique into the equation. This is about forming lasting partnerships with your customers, not landing a one-time sale.

If you are applying sales techniques before establishing an authentic connection with the customer, your partner pyramid is flipped upside down. This is a very precarious position to be in, one with no support— no backing to rely on during those moments when your relationship must stand the test of time and endure obstacles. In fact if you are using sales techniques without an established relationship with the customer, you are selling through manipulation, which is something your customer (and most people) can spot a mile away. The process does not instill trust and feels "off" to the recipient. That is their intuition kicking in. We have all felt that feeling when someone is trying to take advantage of the situation…or even worse, of us. It's unpleasant, isn't it? Would you choose to do business with someone who made you feel that way?

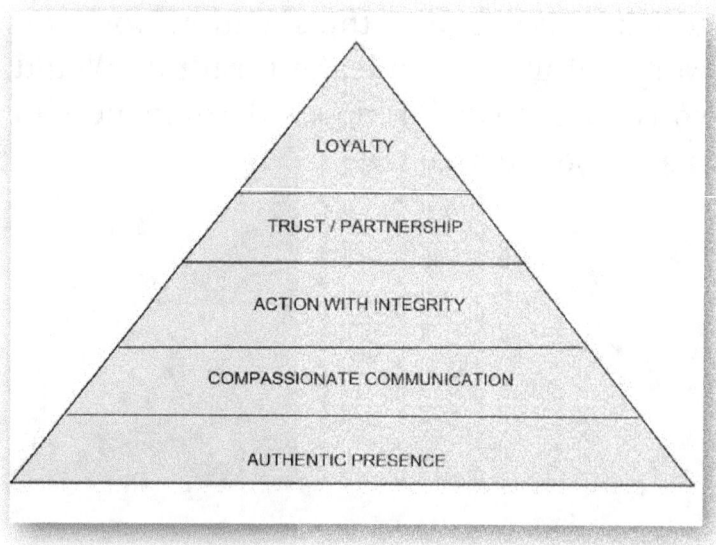

The Partner Pyramid

Before you can begin to create these interactions with your customers, you have to come on the scene with a clean slate. It starts with you. You must be able to present yourself in your entirety, walls down—with authentic, clear communication and a real desire to understand your customer's story first and their needs second—and then have that drive to provide a solution that truly is a win-win.

This is not about someone getting "one up" on another person; this is not even about getting a sale on that day. Sacrilege, I know. This is about joining forces with your customer and being there for them, not out of obligation but out of a passion for what you do and an integrity toward the role you play in that person's success. It's about truly believing that a customer's success is your success and that you are in this together. Without this type of partnership based in trust, you may get a sale out of that customer when you can present the best price, or terms, or available inventory, but anything else is certainly not guaranteed. That customer has the option of buying from any of countless other providers, and you will simply not be able to provide them with what's needed 100 percent of the time.

So here's where the relationship comes in. The goal is to cultivate a relationship with your customers that brings them to you first when there is an opportunity or a need. Where they give you an advantage because they want you to get the business. Where they are loyal to you, value your time together, and think of you as their business partner. This is how you prevent leaving any money on the table—you get the opportunity to fill the need first. If for some reason you can't, the customer will look to a secondary vendor, but the next time around they are right back with you again, the de facto "primary spot holder" they extend the opportunity to first. It's all relationship driven. The "money follows" concept means the relationship comes before the money and ensures that as much of the business as possible gets dropped in your bucket on an ongoing basis.

If you can be open enough to examine yourself and your current customer interactions, along with what those behaviors are rooted in, you can establish the habit of being in the right frame of mind to achieve the level of interaction you want to have with your customers. Your personal pyramid must have a solid and sustaining foundation to build upon, one where you cultivate your own well-being mentally, emotionally, and physically, in order to become an authentic communicator with integrity and values as you reach the pinnacle of trust. You trust in yourself, which leads to trust in others—in turn giving others permission to trust in you. Resolve to be your personal best. Once this is established, you can proceed with creating the type of relationship you want to have with your customers—the type of relationship that leads to fulfillment, loyalty, and long-term partnerships.

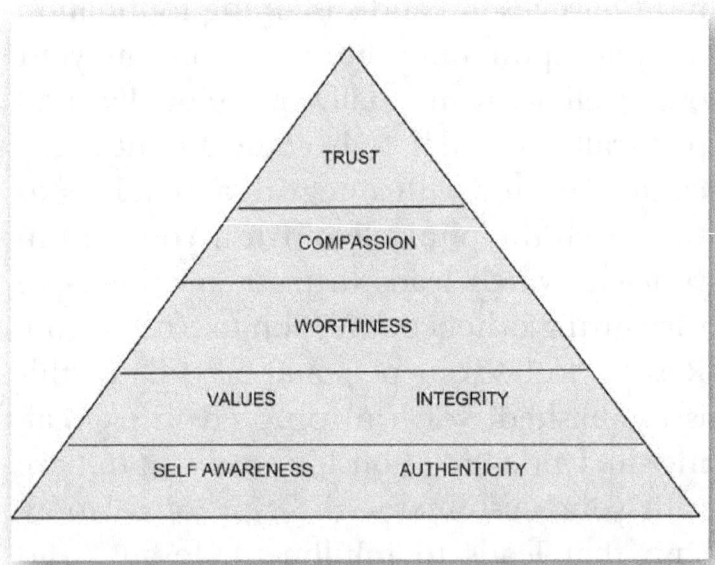

The Personal Pyramid

Get Real

Your reality is frequently inaccurate. What does this mean? It means your thought processes, actions, and very way of being are colored by your beliefs—belief systems that you, as a child and throughout life, have built to avoid feeling loss or discomfort. Your responses to all your combined earlier experiences have very nicely formed a cocoon of sorts that protects you from feeling the full brunt of rejection, humiliation, embarrassment, or any feelings that sting or make you uncomfortable.

What this means, then, is we are all less emotionally vested. We control our levels of engagement, our levels of involvement. We often don't say what we mean because we can sometimes, quite unconsciously, go on autopilot. Have you ever left work and gotten in your car and the next thing you know you're pulling into your driveway? Where did that time go? What was your reality during that drive? Most likely, you were caught up in your thoughts, the brain analyzing a situation "out of body," as they say. Autopilot happens more often than we are aware of…

this lack of presence in the moment. We can even quite unconsciously create situations to prove our old belief systems to be true.

So you may function in your day-to-day life quite sure of your own perspective of "how things are" with no self-awareness of the power you wield in every situation…no awareness that your energy and thoughts and input are creating each and every moment. So the question is, what part of you do you want creating the moments in your life? The protective, abbreviated, autopilot you, or what I like to call the *full press you,* with walls down, true interaction, and authentic presence? Recognizing your delusions is not a sign of weakness but strength personified. When you are *that* real, you are opening the door to greatness.

Sales can be scary business. Walking in cold to attempt to engage a customer takes chutzpah. At that moment you risk rejection, anger, embarrassment…why, just think of everything that could go wrong! Dealing with an unhappy customer is just as daunting. Sales reps are often on the receiving end of customer frustrations; it's part of being the "face" to the customer. Customers not only use us to vent but also have great expectations of their sales reps to fix things, to make things how the customer perceives they should be, whether or not the reps realistically have the power to make that happen.

You are well aware of this from past experiences, and so in true self-preservation mode, you adjust your armor before going in to help deflect whatever comes your way that may make you uncomfortable. The walls come up and the persona goes on and deals with the issue at hand, but this is at the expense of a real and authentic interaction. The persona can manifest itself in various ways, which we look at later. Regardless, the more you do this, the more normal it becomes, sometimes reaching the point where you are doing it even in situations where there is no issue or need to protect yourself—completely unnoticed by you. The point is it keeps you from making true connections. This is the cost of employing protective mechanisms. Simon Sinek, author of

Leaders Eat Last: Why Some Teams Pull Together and Others Don't, notes, "We sometimes have to take on difficult and unreasonable clients, but let's do so consciously."

These coping strategies at some point stop serving you and also stop serving the customer. So it starts with you. Digging deep and finding your awareness toward your own behaviors can only benefit you and, likewise, your relationships with your customers. You might be wondering, *If I am doing this unconsciously, how do I identify when I am doing it?* Developing an awareness of your self-talk (that little voice in your head) is an important first step. Listen to the things you sometimes say to yourself. Would you speak that way to a loved one? To a child? To an elderly or sickly person? Never. You would surely make an effort to approach any subject with kindness and compassion, not with the harsh words and unforgiving judgment you can sometimes unleash on yourself.

In *When Things Fall Apart: Heart Advice for Difficult Times,* author Pema Chödrön notices, "The most difficult times for many of us are those we give ourselves." Accepting and loving all parts of yourself, including those aspects you might deem as flaws, takes a personal commitment and follow through. It sounds so simple, and it really is. Think of it as an immediate pivot at the moment you become aware of a self-destructive or fear-based thought process. Stop and reframe your thoughts in a more positive tone. Literally replace a negative thought about any situation with a positive thought—a negative with a positive. Make this a habit. Show yourself the utmost compassion, understanding that only this will allow you freedom to live fluidly and without fear. Freedom to grow and expand, freedom to "knock it out of the park"—that's the mentality. Accept your flaws and weaknesses, and commit to improve in areas where you feel you could benefit from some growth.

Fully accept your talents, what you're great at. Accept your worthiness. Be bold and courageous. Identify your true values, and commit to living by them. An interesting experiment is to write your own obituary.

How would you like it to read? What would you like people to say about you? Were you kind, courageous, authentic, a person of integrity, honest, and helpful to others? Could you be counted on? Were you reliable by nature? Suddenly, the values that are important to you start to surface.

I have repeated the use of the word *commit* in this section, and it's an important one. Keeping commitments to yourself is one of the first steps to living authentically. Developing a level of trust with yourself is pertinent to anyone else trusting you. This isn't willpower we're talking about; this is caring enough about yourself to keep promises you've made. Integrity toward yourself is a visible quality to those around you and instills trust in how you, in turn, will act with them. It lets others know that you can be counted on.

Try to identify what emotional payoffs you might be getting from choosing (consciously or not) *not* to live your values, choosing *not* to live your best life. Maybe you can identify with this: "Well, I didn't try my best, so it really wasn't my fault things didn't work out." It might sound nonsensical; however, this is how the mind can analyze a situation and put into place coping mechanisms in an attempt to protect you. What about "I held back, I didn't go for it, so I was prepared for the poor results"? Of course it wasn't going to work out; that was your expectation, so now you're not disappointed. "My expectations of myself were easily met. If I would have chosen to give it my all, it may have had a different outcome, but that didn't happen, so now I can (and will) attribute the failure to any number of other things."

No? OK, how about doing things to gain approval, albeit for the wrong reasons, sometimes referred to as "people pleasing." Think about the emotional payoff you get from feeling approval, regardless of whether it is deserved or whether you actually gained it through authentic actions that were true to your core values. We are thirsty for approval in any form, even when it is dysfunctional. It's an instant gratification that says, "You're good enough," or perhaps, "You're the best," even when the reasons are hollow and not backed up by reality. These ego boosts are not free. There is usually a cost for inauthentic actions down the road, but the ego also has a talent for ignoring that impending situation too.

Now let's really get down to the bones: "Not doing my best proves the lies I tell myself to be true, and I would rather have that feeling because it's comfortable in its own way and self-examination, risk, and change are uncomfortable and scary." If none of this resonates with you, you may also just be at a point where you don't feel anything in particular or you don't feel everything, and I will let you decide for yourself which of those is worse. Fear of failure can play a part in these types of avoidance behaviors, and fear will sometimes show up as procrastination, which causes guilt and shame.

Allowing yourself to fail sometimes is an important step in personal growth and gaining knowledge. In Pema Chödrön's book *Fail, Fail Again, Fail Better: Wise Advice for Leaning into the Unknown,* she discusses finding the opportunity in failure: "Failing better means when these things happen in your life, they become a source of growth, a source of forward, a source of out of that place of rawness you can really communicate genuinely with other people." When you can open your perspective enough to be able to view your failures as possible positives in life's experience, it removes the fear and anxiety you may currently associate with the level of effort that's being asked of you. It gives you the freedom to grow and change and stay fluid, to try new things and have different perspectives. It encourages you to communicate openly and also encourages others to be open with you. This is a ripple effect that moves the relationship forward while at the same time strengthening its base. Acknowledge your feelings and fears in order to process them and move on. It just takes the awareness of the fear or belief and the action of questioning it ("Is that true?") to start unraveling its hold. Another great questioning process with yourself that quells fear and anxiety is the "and then what" method. Start with the most worrisome thought and assume it happens. Ask yourself, "And then what happens?" Your mind will likely supply you with another bad thing that might result. Ask again, "And then what happens?" Continue down this path until you get to the worst-case scenario. Surprisingly, you will typically find that no one dies in the end, no one's life gets ruined, and in fact it's usually something you could handle. Just like that, the fear is lessened. You have faced it and decided you will live. Great. Now move forward.

The Evil Twins

Now might be a good time to address the "evil twins" in our lives: comparison and perfectionism. It has been said that comparison is the thief of joy. This holds true in today's environment. Constantly comparing yourself and your accomplishments to others will never result in fulfillment or happiness. Quite the opposite, it will keep you in a state of feeling either inferior (which is a delusion and a lie we tell ourselves) or superior (which as it turns out isn't so great for your psyche either). It's alienating and constantly needs reaffirming. The need to feel superior also can easily lead to the mistreatment of others. In both cases, it is self-defeating and a hugely negative and exhausting way to live.

Authentic living is never about measuring up against others and looking to knock them down to better position yourself. You must live with so much integrity and belief in yourself that you would never consider doing that. It's about doing what you can to elevate others at the same time you cultivate your own ability to transform and grow in your environment. Ernest Hemingway said, "There is nothing noble in being superior to your fellow man; true nobility is being superior to your former self." Be content with where you are, yet never stop growing. Practice gratitude and appreciation for the road already traveled, for all the obstacles you have found your way through, around, and over. Appreciate your perseverance, and congratulate yourself on your life skills. Do not assume that the exterior appearance of another's situation is correct; instead, it's more likely another misperception of reality on your part, otherwise known as "the grass is always greener." Author Scott Barry Kaufman in a piece for *Scientific American* conducted a core-tenets-of-character-strengths analysis and found that *the single best predictor of well-being was gratitude.* We can always be appreciative, without exception. Make a habit of acknowledging the good things in every day. Some days it might be the air in your lungs, and other days it will be overwhelming how many good things you can tally up. Typically, the list grows as your awareness of the positive becomes a habit. It is in this way that you cultivate gratitude, which leads to fulfillment, hope, happiness, and well-being. Once you have this insight, it will help you get through changing times or challenges you will sometimes experience in your field of work. It can be easy to feel alone in facing obstacles that inevitably come your way. If you have the level of power to readjust what is not working, by all means make that your focus. At times, however, a sales rep can be at the mercy of the internal workings of their company or any number of external forces in play. While it may be your first instinct to feel frustration at what is "not working," if you have no control over changing that, you have no business focusing on it. Deal with it as you must when it comes your way, and give the proper channels your feedback on the matter. Then immediately turn your thoughts and energies back to what *is* working at that time. And know that, without exception, all others in your profession suffer similar obstacles at one time or another. Sustain yourself through it.

If you're guaranteed one thing, it's that things never stay the same for very long. Be fluid in a fluid business environment; initiate personal growth during periods of your company's growth. Become so stable internally that you are simultaneously flexible. It's the ultimate paradox. I sometimes remind myself that I've been through worse, so this particular problem on its own is not going to make or break me—of this I can be sure. This helps me give it the right level of importance in my life, personally or professionally, because as we know, these two bleed together at times. Work ethic and discipline are always in play in the background, but the goal is to embody or become the type of salesperson (or person) you want to be and not have to work so hard at it. This means being so authentic that it wouldn't even make sense to compare your unique self to someone else. It wouldn't be comparing apples to apples. Authenticity doesn't require a struggle, only a level of honesty with one's self, followed by compassionate acceptance and the right intentions.

Likewise, perfectionism is, in all reality, an unachievable goal. To strive for perfectionism is to work toward something you will never accomplish. Framing your goals in such a way causes creative constriction, procrastination, and feelings of lack and defeat. Do you usually cross off everything on your to-do list? If you're like the rest of us (and you are), things get bumped to the next day, and such is life—progressive, not perfect. It's more important to put yourself out there, flaws and all, and actually take action than it is to plan for a perfect offering at the perfect time. High work standards should, of course, be the norm, but keep in mind that taking action trumps making mistakes. We have to be willing to be wrong, solicit feedback, correct our course, and start again. This is the learning process for all new things in your life: no judgment, only progress. As the saying goes, "Mistakes are proof you are trying." Practice living fearlessly.

Interesting fact: children learn to walk before they've developed logical thinking. This is because learning to walk requires exploration without the constraint of their little brains telling them, "This can't possibly work! Stay down on all fours! It's much safer there! You are closer to the ground if you fall! The risk...it's too much!" No, there's none of that. Nature has ensured that babies blissfully use their intuition to get up on two feet, stumble and fall, find support, and try again, until one day they are victorious as they toddle across the room on their own. Think more like a toddler.

> *And now that you don't have*
> *to be perfect, you can be good.*
> —*JOHN STEINBECK,* EAST OF EDEN

Our deepest fear is not that we are inadequate. Our deepest fear is that we are powerful beyond measure. It is our light, not our darkness that most frightens us. We ask ourselves, Who am I to be brilliant, gorgeous, talented, fabulous? Actually, who are you not to be? You are a child of God. Your playing small doesn't serve the world. There is nothing enlightened about shrinking so that other people won't feel insecure around you. We are all meant to shine, as children do. We were born to make manifest the glory of God that is within us. It's not just in some of us; it's in everyone. And as we let our own light shine, we unconsciously give other people permission to do the same. As we are liberated from our own fear, our presence automatically liberates others.
—MARIANNE WILLIAMSON,
A RETURN TO LOVE

It's Right in the Word

Selling through the lens of compassion may sound too soft in the competitive world of sales, where one-upmanship and personal gain typically take precedence, but there's something you may be missing about the concept—*passion*. It's right in the word. There is no compassion without passion: a passion for living your values, for being your best self; a passion for servicing your customers; a passion for creating the best outcome for all involved. All compassionate acts! The power of having passion for what you do is your trump card. Moving your perspective on your career from obligation to passion is a game changer. Choosing to come from a place of honor and compassion is an instant antidote for job stagnation. It takes an awareness of how you feel and focused intention.

Your emotions are real and right on the money 100 percent of the time, unlike your thoughts. Connect to your emotions, and use them as your compass. It is the subtle difference of wanting something (brain driven) and desiring something (emotion driven).

In his TED Talk "Why We Do What We Do," Tony Robbins addressed Al Gore, who was sitting in the audience. Gore had spoken at the TED conference an evening prior about his true passion, climate change and the environment. "If you showed the same passion and energy as we saw last night during the presidential debates, you would have beaten that guy," Robbins said. Gore's passion for the subject at hand brought out his authentic self. His speeches were filled with emotion and genuine interaction with his audiences. And yes, he was vulnerable. He was putting himself out there. The legitimacy of climate change data, particularly at the time the movie *An Inconvenient Truth* came out, was still being questioned and denied by many. How was he able to put himself in such a vulnerable position after suffering such a public loss with his bid for the presidency? Passion overrode fear.

Think of compassion as a verb, an action you consciously take…an intention you start each day with, to have compassion first and foremost for yourself. "If your compassion does not include yourself, it is incomplete," said Jack Kornfield in *Buddha's Little Instruction Book*. Having the courage to put yourself in the vulnerable position of changing your mind-set, or belief, about how sales is done builds self-worth on its own. You're master of your own destiny, creating your life instead of merely being a participant. You're empowered.

> *There is no passion to be found in settling for a life that is less than the one you are capable of living.*
> —NELSON MANDELA

PART 3

SUSTAINABLE PARTNERSHIPS

Hidden Costs

How would a lack of compassion toward yourself and your customers affect your customer relationships? The results speak for themselves. It would create an inability to have authentic interactions on your (the sales rep's) part, resulting in a lack of connection with the customer. It would block trust, authentic and meaningful communication, and any chances of a loyal, long-term partnership. It would make you just another vendor selling the same stuff everyone else is. Your relationships would be based on price and product availability and would be expendable. You would be easily replaceable. Suddenly, the willingness to be vulnerable and create these new paradigms with your customers doesn't seem so radical. It makes sense for everyone involved.

Let's dig deeper and put some metrics on it. What is the going cost of replacing a lost customer? In many ways the metric assigned to the loss of an existing customer is immeasurable. There are intangibles involved. But looking at some stats will help us understand why sustainable customer relationships hold the importance they do in today's business world.

Ivor Jones, chairman of ThinkSales Corporation, takes a look at *The Real Cost of Losing Customers*:

- Around 68 percent of customer defection takes place because customers feel poorly treated.
- A whopping 95 percent of people who have a bad experience do not complain.
- Around 13 percent of unhappy customers tell up to twenty other people, while a satisfied customer tells only five other people.
- It can cost five times more to gain new customers than to retain existing ones.
- A 1 percent cut in customer service issues could generate an extra two hundred million in profits for a medium-size company over five years.
- A lost customer always creates an opportunity for the competition.

Conversely, long-term customer relation-ships increase the profitability of a company. Less marketing expenditures means more opportunity at category penetration and high dollar sales. A company's most valuable asset is its customer base. It is often the only sustainable source of direct income into the company. Long-term customers tend to buy less on price and more on relationship. Their average order sizes are higher. They require fewer internal resources and tend to be crea-tures of habit, meaning they are somewhat predictable, making things easier on you and your company. This does not mean you can "autopilot" them. In fact, maintaining and growing existing business should be part of your growth strategy for your territory. This requires regular interaction and attention, letting customers know you are there for them and they and their business are impor-tant to you.

Cultivating loyalty isn't the only thing that's important here. This is also about nur-turing those customer relationships in order to uncover all available possibilities within the partnership—it's about not leaving money on the table that could be directed to you. This requires high levels of communication and truly understanding your customers' needs, as well as the function of their positions, the ideals of their companies, and their specific processes. These are the things a true business partner would educate themselves on.

You want to be constantly gaining insight about your customers and how they are personally vested, as well as on how their organizations work as a whole. Their pain is your pain. Speaking of pain, have you ever noticed how many sales-technique acronyms encourage selling by unveiling pain to the customer or using fear of liability? These fall under the category of inauthenticity and manipulation in my book, and truly, they are no longer necessary. Educating your customers about a possible liability by way of concern for their business is something different than presenting a veiled threat. Always come from a position of authenticity and compassion. Fear-based sales are not sustainable, and they never were.

Real vs. Fake

Before discussing authentic sales, we must first identify very clearly what inauthentic selling looks like. One of my least favorite things on earth is being sold. Someone trying to sell me something with even a whiff of inauthenticity puts my hair on end. It's the worst when a salesperson simply assumes what my needs are or overtly tries to manipulate me into doing what he or she wants with no regard to what I may want at the moment. Not only do I not want to interact with this person, but I really want to remove myself from the situation at the soonest opportunity.

I recently participated in a group conversation about inauthentic selling. One of the group members related that she was feeling some guilt about her behavior with a salesperson earlier in the day. She admittedly was not having a great day and had gone into a high end shoe store to look around. She was immediately approached by a salesman asking if he could help her find anything. She declined his assistance, saying she just wanted to browse. His very next interaction with her involved sidling up to her a second time and asking, "Hey, what's your name?" She was so thrown off by his inauthentic attempt at intimacy and clear manipulative intentions that she immediately left the store. "What's the big deal?" you might say. "He was trying to make a connection." But isn't it interesting how little it takes to make someone feel put off.

The bottom line is he wasn't asking for her name out of true interest in her; this was a smarmy shortcut to get him where he wanted to be. He had two other good options: one, leave her alone to shop for a while as she asked (staying available to help when she was ready), and the other, a genuine second attempt to approach her on an authentic level. Most likely, if the salesman had paid attention to her verbal cues, her expressions, her body language, and her energy, it would have been evident that she maybe wasn't having the best day of her life, and he could have easily picked up on that and gone from there. I submit that a bit of tweaking in his second conversation could have changed the entire feel of the scene. Imagine if he had made eye contact, let her know he was available to her, and maybe made a lighthearted statement about how an amazing pair of shoes always saves the day. The difference is clear. This time it was about her and acknowledging her feelings, assessing her needs at that moment. He would have then come across as an ally instead of someone who was trying to get something out of her for personal benefit.

Granted, retail sales is its own animal, and the retail salesperson must work in a much smaller window of time than those in a sales position involving a sales cycle, site visits, and meetings with various levels of personnel where there is an opportunity to value the person's time and show up with an authentic level of presence. What does this mean? As discussed earlier, it means showing up with your walls down and 100 percent of your attention focused on the other person. It means reading body language, sensing feelings, listening to the person's story, and absorbing it before responding. "Listening to respond" is one of the most common mistakes made in sales. There is a reason that "silent" and "listen" are composed of the same letters: they go hand in hand. What's that old saying in sales? Something about "He who speaks first after an offer is on the table loses"? It's the same idea. People need time to integrate conversations and ideas.

We live in a time where instant gratification often necessitates a frantic pace of communicating. We have so much to say, so many solutions to offer, that we just can't wait for the other person to stop talking so we can dump it all on the table. This listening tactic, however, doesn't allow for devoted attention to what the other person is saying or the space you need to decipher what the true underlying need may be. An authentic sense of presence is calm, attentive, focused, and discerning…not attaching to all the perceptions and thoughts your brain may be throwing at you in that moment. You don't always have to give an immediate answer. A level of presence like this gives the other person permission to be present with you too. People will only feel comfortable letting their walls down when they don't feel barraged or manipulated. When the energy of the interaction is calm and helpful, they feel heard and understood.

> *There's nothing people won't tell you if you ask in a compassionate and legitimately interested way.*
> — BRANDON STANTON,
> HUMANS OF NEW YORK

Will all customers respond in kind to being offered such an open avenue of communication? Will they know what to do with it? Not all of them. But I want you to start imagining having built loyal and sustainable partnerships with even a third of your current customer base. What would look different about that as compared to today? Move toward the goal more each and every day, and watch that percentage grow in your favor.

I have a masseuse I am very loyal to, and I was thinking about *why* I held such loyalty toward her. She's a good enough masseuse, but that wasn't what made me postpone my massages until I could get in with her. What secured me as "her" client was that I felt like she really cared about what my experience was in any given moment. The front desk at this place had its struggles and was always leaving me waiting too long, forgetting to tell her I was there, and those types of things. The second she walked on the scene, she was laser focused on me. She would protectively hustle me away into the back, fending off zealous front desk personnel trying to get me to fill out a form for the third time. She would always acknowledge my unpleasant experience and say, "Now don't you worry about any of that. You just relax. This is your time."

She would always sit with me first, asking about my health and how my body was feeling that day. She would assess what my issues were and address them directly through massage techniques. Sometimes she would offer me tokens as compensation of sorts for my having been forgotten about, or whatever the issue du jour was with the check-in process—maybe incorporate hot stones during the massage or some aromatherapy, or add some extra minutes onto my session. These were things that were *within her power to do* and that didn't cost her much, if anything at all, but her acknowledgment of the situation alone made me feel happy. *I felt cared for.* Also, she never took both hands off me at once. At a minimum, she would leave just two fingers lightly touching my arm while she moved around the table or retrieved something from the shelf. She never broke physical connection with me. It said, "I'm here with you. My attention is still on you."

Now, I'm not suggesting that you touch your customers, although a good handshake speaks volumes, but it's the concept of being *that* present with a customer in every moment you spend with him or her that is so powerful. Your attention is always right there, focused on the customer. You're hearing and processing everything that person is saying. You are detecting hidden or unexpressed needs by understanding what the person's story is on that particular day. You're invested. Your phone is on silent. You're not looking at your phone when a call comes in and certainly never answering a call. (If you answer a call during a meeting with a customer, you might as well say, "Hold on, this person is more important than you are to me.") You're not thinking about your last sales visit or feeling preoccupied with an upcoming deal that you need to sort out the details on. You are calm, centered, focused, and present with your customer in every moment. This is the customer's time. They don't call it the "customer experience" for nothing.

It's sometimes difficult for people to be receptive to an attempt at authentic presence if there is no existing trust established because they are worried about being taken advantage of. Yet it's paradoxical because this is the very foundation of the formula in building trust with a partner. There is an alchemy to it. You must start with presence and compassionate communications, followed by integrity in your actions. You lead your customers along the path to trust. You earn it. You need to have that clear intention.

You are in the driver's seat to create all of this with your customer. You are cultivating customer loyalty because loyalty follows trust very naturally and is at the pinnacle of the partner pyramid. It is your ultimate goal in all of your customer relationships.

Let's talk about integrity for a minute. *Merriam-Webster* defines *integrity* as "the quality of being honest and fair; adherence to moral and ethical principles; soundness of character." The root word of *integrity* is the Latin adjective *integer*, meaning "whole or complete," used to describe an *inner sense of wholeness*. Why is this important, and how does it play into sustainable partnerships with your customers?

Integrity is an immediately recognized quality in those who have it, just as it is blatant and obvious when someone lacks integrity. A person with integrity is going to do what they say, fulfill commitments, and be invested in win-win situations in negotiations. A person with integrity doesn't have a hidden agenda or a false sense of bravado, doesn't make excuses when they make a mistake. A person with integrity isn't just in it for the money. Even the phrase "in it for the money" carries a negative connotation, and for good reason. If you aren't interested in anything but making the immediate sale, you're more likely to use questionable tactics to get there. When a customer feels you are more interested in being a business partner than in getting their money, the battle is won. It's all you from then on. The money will follow, and it will be sustainable.

The long and short of things is that you can count on people with integrity; they are reliable. So when you approach everything you do with a sense of integrity and your actions bear this out, you create a comfort level in the people around you, and it encourages them to partner with you. They don't feel like they constantly have to be watching you, or following up, or protecting their interests. They are comfortable knowing you will do the right thing. Be honorable; have a sense of honor. Wear it on your sleeve. It's such a rare and precious commodity these days, and people assign tremendous value to it.

Award-winning million-dollar mentors Jesse Koren and Sharla Jacobs write about and teach the "Heartselling" way of sales. In their book *The Art of Attracting Clients,* they discuss this heart-based sales methodology. I was fortunate to be able to interview Sharla recently about the concept. "If you are looking to establish a long-term relationship with a client, you want that trust to be built in and for it to be solid," Sharla says. "Selling through fear and manipulation will cause that relationship to start off on a negative note, and it will turn at some point. Heartselling is essentially an inspiring conversation that leads to action." In their book Jesse and Sharla contend that *sell* is actually a five-letter word spelled *s-e-r-v-e.* "How do you serve? You find out if what they are looking for is something you can help them with before you launch into your spiel about what you do."

Listening to your customers is paramount. Make sure you are not walking in and pre-supposing their needs. Your customers' needs will vary and change over time, and you're no mind reader. Have a natural sense of curiosity, as discussed further in *The Art of Attracting Clients*: "When you take time to get curious about your...clients, it shows you are interested and they will feel like someone cares about them. When you express genuine curiosity, it creates trust."

What are the things that may make us appear inauthentic to others? Inauthentic speech can be something that taps your customer on the shoulder and makes them feel something toward you, something that says you are not to be taken at face value, your words are not always to be trusted. It only takes one time where a customer notices that something you said maybe was not entirely real or honest to put everything else you've ever said to them into question.

Employing sarcasm and putting down competitors are part of inauthentic speech. There are other aspects that seem harmless, such as a tendency to exaggerate ("I've done this a hundred times before."), being self-congratulatory or boasting ("I'm a player; you know I got this!"), or being overly charming and smarmy. Even a habit of constantly joking can come across as inauthentic, as customers don't know when to take you seriously. It's fine—great, in fact—to have a sense of humor or the ability to bring lightheartedness into play when it's a fit to the situation. Constantly hiding behind the mask of comedy, however, looks like just that—wearing a mask.

The point is people pick up on these language idiosyncrasies. We live in a world where people crave authenticity over artifice. Make it your intention every day to be clear and accurate in your speech and true to your word. Have the confidence to not stoop to degenerating your competition. Let your actions speak for themselves. If you're good, you don't have to go around telling everyone that you're good and someone else is bad. It's just self-evident.

So what, then, does an authentic sale look like? It starts with eye contact and an appreciative handshake. Let's consider your handshake for a moment. Think about how you would take a family member's or a loved one's hand and give it a reassuring squeeze that says,

"I'm here for you, I support you, and I care about you." This is the same pressure you want to have with a customer. Don't overdo it or let it go on too long; don't squeeze too firmly or shake with a relaxed hand. These all send different messages with negative connotations.

If you really want to impress, master the two-handed handshake. Place your other hand over the back side of your customer's hand, so you are holding the customer's hand with both of your hands during the shake. This sends an instant message to the customer's brain that you are both welcoming and can be trusted. Variations that are progressively more familiar are placing your free hand on the customer's forearm while shaking hands or, in the most familiar, on the corresponding shoulder. It's a connection, and probably the only physical connection you will have with your customers. Treat it as a bonding moment. It may seem like the least of what you should be working on, but let's face it, you're in sales. You need a good solid handshake to break out at a moment's notice. Be aware of your execution of it.

Also be conscious that you are not coming from a place of obligation. We all have tasks and interactions we don't necessarily cherish, but a partnership is created out of genuine interest and personal investment. Your customers' businesses should feel like your businesses. Fulfilling your customers' needs and providing them with solutions should give you a feeling of accomplishment, and the journey there should be seen as your creation, a chance to demonstrate your expertise, a chance to learn more about your industry and how it functions, a chance to positively impact another human being. Loving your job should be the standard, not the exception. Understand the value you can bring to everyone you touch. You are not doing mindless work, assembling parts, or inputting data. You are fortunate enough to have the freedom to be creative in your job, to come up with ideas and solutions that directly affect your customers' levels of success. Be enthusiastic. Be grateful every night for what you were able to accomplish, and release what you were not. You will try again tomorrow with a fresh slate.

When you cultivate this attitude and approach customer interactions from this perspective, you will be creating a positive and authentic environment, both for yourself and for those you come in contact with. Find something to admire and appreciate about each customer. You don't have to share these thoughts with your customers; this is just for you to recognize and acknowledge and to remember when you are with them. Don't forget, appreciation of any kind quickly gains momentum.

As for the sales conversation, we have already discussed the importance of having a strong level of presence and openness with your customers while practicing solid listening skills. Observe and retain everything you can about what is and isn't working for your customer, where that customer is vested, and what outcome he or she desires. Take copious notes. Nothing makes me more nervous than telling someone something containing detail and having that person look at me and nod but take no notes. Unless the person has a photographic memory, I don't trust that they are going to remember all the detail and nuances of the conversation. Taking notes is also a huge indicator to the customer that you are truly listening and that you place importance on what they are saying. Having said this, be careful that you aren't hiding behind a laptop screen or giving your computer more eye contact than your customer. Whatever your note-taking mode of choice is, make sure it's not the star of the show. Keep it off to the side or down low on your lap so as not to create a physical obstacle between you and the customer.

Give attention to people's body language; read between the lines. Intuiting a customer's true needs is a developed skill that starts with you giving your undivided attention to all aspects of your customer's sharings. Even customers who appear to be extremely forthright and sometimes aggressive in their communications have backstories. Actually, especially those people. Like a detective, it's up to you to nail and decipher those clues. Ask relevant questions to peel away the layers. Once you're through with this "discovery" part of the conversation, it may be time to talk resources, ideas, and solutions, with closing in mind. Or maybe not. Depending on the circumstances, it might be more beneficial to stop there and agree to reconvene after you have done some research, found some resources, or simply thought it through more. It's a sales *cycle*—the term itself indicates a process. Don't jump to conclusions before you are clear on what the best course of action is for you and your customer. Your goal should always be to create a situation that is win-win. You're looking for a solid win for you and your company and a great progressive solution for your customer.

It is your job to act as an expert in your industry, to educate customers about how your offerings fit their needs. Remember, there is a difference between educating and fear mongering. So many sales techniques play on a customer's fears, but again, if you are the real deal, this just isn't necessary. As discussed earlier, liability is a conversation you should have if it is pertinent, but selling based on fear of liability starts to cross over into the inauthentic sales arena. Even if the liability is an acceptable reason for the customer to buy something, you would be better served presenting it in an educational way instead of a "what would happen if" kind of way. You are not here to scare or intimidate the customer into doing business with you; you are here to help them, for goodness sake! You want the customer to feel supported, not give them anxiety. The result is the same, so it's a cheap shortcut to make the customer feel uneasy so you can close a sale.

Let's not forget our value and worth. Manipulation in sales is like using your big dumb muscles. Refine your conversations. The earned and valuable skills you have should not be sullied by accessing and using questionable practices, ever. Again, it only takes one questionable interaction for the customer to always feel like they need to keep an eye on you. It always comes down to the little things when you are building trust.

Trust You Me

My father owned an appliance rental and repair business when I was growing up. When he first started the business, our family had just moved from Michigan across the country to California. He was unestablished with no customer base. Over the years the business became very successful, supporting our family of nine, and he kept it until he retired. He used to tell me when I was young, "Do you know how I let people know they could trust me? If I ever found change in the dryer I was fixing, I left it on top of the machine. Soon, repeat customers started leaving me a key so I could enter and complete the job even when they weren't home. Then it became easy for them to use me." Fifty-six cents on top of a dryer built a foundation of trust. He also was known to give young, struggling families free used washers or dryers when the need presented itself. People knew he cared about them and their situations, and his success naturally followed. I suppose he did a pretty good job of fixing appliances too, but I've never once heard anyone talk about that skill specifically when they've mentioned him. Lots of people can fix an appliance. My father was welcomed into these people's lives and homes. Although he is no longer here with us, to this day I will run into people who came into contact with my dad, and there is always a story about how he was helpful to them in some way. That's what trust can do. It's the little things that build a legacy.

What makes a customer trust you? Philosopher Onora O'Neill, in her TED Talk "What We Don't Understand About Trust," notes, "If you make yourself vulnerable to the other party, then that is very good evidence that you are trustworthy." In addition, you will want to work toward creating a proven track record of results that were always customer-centric. Employ strong follow-up skills, and be efficient yet effective. Do what you say, without exception. Own up to mistakes, and fix them right away; don't brush them under the rug or try to assign blame. Mistakes can embarrass us, and our initial reactions may be to dodge and weave. Don't let a mistake define you for longer than it takes to fix it. Rather, do everything in your power to make sure something similar doesn't happen again. Communicate how you have corrected your course to ensure that is the case. Be impassioned, compassionate, forgiving. Live by your core values, have integrity, be strong, and have a quiet inner strength that is so strong it is unflappable. A calm sense of composure in all situations yields the best results and tells your customer, "I have this under control."

Handle things with grace. Be someone your customers want in their corner. Never argue with the customer or become emotional. This is not what impassioned means. The problem is irrelevant; it's your response that matters. A measure of a person's character is how he or she handles disappointments. How quickly do you get up and dust yourself off and keep moving forward? Watch that your ingrained responses don't bubble up quickly in difficult situations. Breathe through it. You always have your breath. Three deep, slow, intentional breaths taken around a corner or in your car can slow everything right down and ground you so you can proceed without emotion or anger. Relax your jaw, straighten your back, and drop your shoulders. Adopt an even tone of voice, and proceed. The customer is watching your every move, and your actions and attitude are telling them everything they need to know about you. It's up to you to be the person your customer wants to come to.

Partnerships are not created in a vacuum; they are cultivated through connection. There will be ups and downs and variables in all partnerships, but all customers need to know is that you will be there working for their best interests no matter the situation. That you will not abandon them when things get sticky, but you will forge forward with dignity in the most stressful of situations. A sales career can be volatile; it is an inevitability. Allow what is to be. It is the perfection of imperfection. Accepting this reality and having the utmost trust in yourself and your abilities takes courage.

Courage is the most important of all virtues because without courage, you can't practice any other virtue consistently.
— MAYA ANGELOU

A customer should never see you walking up and think, *I'm going to get asked for an order. That rep wants to sell me something today.* That person should see you and think, *The cavalry! My rep is going to help me with something today.* You will know this is working when the customer has notes on things he or she has been keeping to review with you. You will know this is working when the customer calls you first. You will know this is working when a customer is genuinely interested in and respects your opinion. You will know this is working when you maintain primary status with a customer for years on end. You will know this is working when your customers refer you to other customers. You will know this is working when the money follows.

Have courage, kind hearts. You are consummate sales professionals. You have agency. Move forward with compassion, and create your legacy.

NOTES

Part 2

1. Simon Sinek, "Leaders Eat Last," *Success.* (July 2014): n.p. http://www.success.com.

2. Pema Chödrön, "Pith Advice from an American Buddhist Nun: Collected Sayings of Pema Chödrön ," *Elephant Journal,* (September 2013), n.p. http://www.elephantjournal.com.

3. Pema Chödrön, "How to Move Forward Once You've Hit Bottom," *Lion's Roar,* (August 2015), n.p. http://www.lionsroar.com.

4. Tejvan Pettinger, "Ernest Hemingway Biography," *Biography Online* (n.d.): n.p., http://www.biographyonline.net.

5. Scott Barry Kaufman, "Which Character Strengths Are Most Predictive of Well Being," *Scientific American: Beautiful Minds*

(August 2015): n.p., http://blogs.scientificamerican.com.

6. Tony Robbins, "Why We Do What We Do," *TED* (February 2006), http://www.ted.com/talks.

7. Jack Kornfield, *Buddha's Little Instruction Book* (New York: Bantam Books, 1994), page 28.

Part 3
1. Ivor Jones, "The Real Cost of Losing Customers," *ThinkSales* (n.d.): n.p., http://www.thinksales.co.za.

2. Sharla Jacobs (Phone interview, August 2015).

3. Jesse Koren and Sharla Jacobs, *The Art of Attracting Clients* (Santa Cruz: Thrive Academy, 2008), page 41

4. Koren and Jacobs, *The Art of Attracting Clients*

5. Onora O'Neill, "What We Don't Under stand about Trust," *TED* (June 2013), https://www.ted.com/talks.